To: Heather Leigh Hauck
October, 1978

in the same series:

the butterfly book of MAMMALS
the butterfly book of BIRDS
PLAINS INDIANS of North America
IN MY GARDEN (learning to count)
THE FOUR SEASONS
LITTLE RED RIDING HOOD
THE THREE BEARS
HIDDEN IN THE MEADOW

TWO CONTINENTS

31, Quai Anatole-France 75007 Paris ·

Gerda Muller Résie Pouyanne

what I see

hidden by

the Pond

Butterfly Books

pseudo acorus
The marsh iris
is a friend to gnats,
who feast on its nectar.

typha
The bulrush is soft to touch,
and its little catkin
point doesn't scratch.

podiceps

The great crested grebe lives, sleeps and makes its nest on the water. Here Papa Grebe takes one of his babies on a ride near the nest.

caltha

The marsh marigold lights the pond with its bright, sunny color.

myosotis apula

Look closely at the forget-me-not. Little by little, its tiny pink buds unfold into blue flowers.

alcedo

A blue flash on the water, the kingfisher leaves its hidden riverbank nest to look for food.

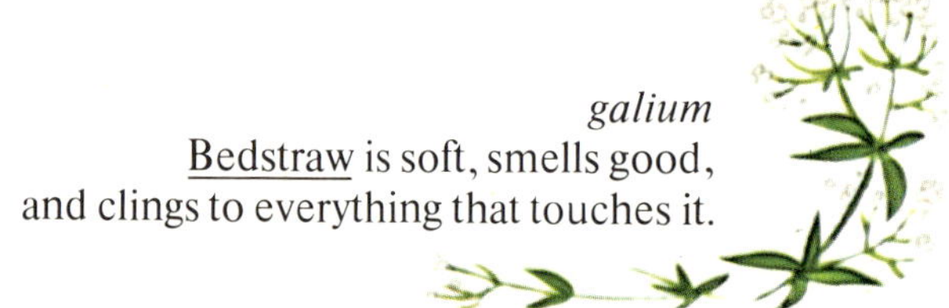

galium

Bedstraw is soft, smells good, and clings to everything that touches it.

libellula

Lady Dragonfly dances in the sunlight after spending two whole years under the water, growing from a larva to a graceful winged insect.

juncus

Rushes are pliable, round reeds, which can be woven into baskets and rugs.

ardea
The heron slowly beats its long broad wings and sails over the pond.
In the evening it hides in the reeds and catches fish for its supper.

sylvia
The reed warbler makes its nest right on the reeds.
This little bird is not easy to see, but you can hear its song.

mentha
The water mint has a lovely fragrance and taste, different from peppermint candies and drinks, which are made from dried mint leaves, grown in gardens.

spirea
The meadowsweet is oddly named, since a big whiff of its smell can be sickening. In bygone times it was called "goat's beard".

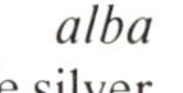

alba
The minnow has scales that shine like silver
out of water, and is sometimes called a shiner.

rana
The tadpole is just a head when it emerges from its egg.
Gradually it grows feet, becomes a frog,
and can jump way out of the water,
to hop around the shore.

sagitta

In the water, the arrowhead's long leaves float like ribbons;
in the air they stand up straight as pointed arrows.

hottonia

The water violet, with its pinkish flowers,
is also called "feather-foil",
because its soft petals
come off at the lightest touch.

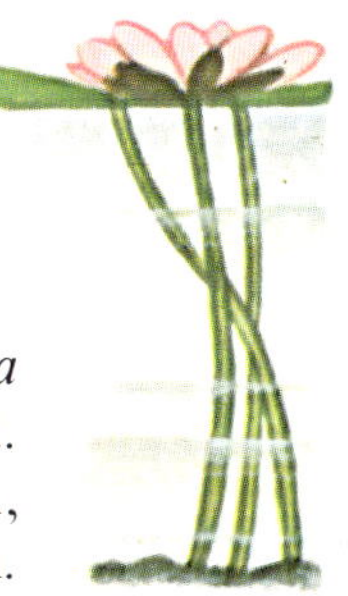

nymphea

Water lilies are attached by their stems to the bottom of the pond.
On the surface, their flat round leaves and full pink,
white and yellow blossoms make a pretty decoration.

gallinula
The water-hen or coot usually lays about ten eggs, colored yellow with brown spots. When her babies are hatched, she teaches them to swim fast and dive underwater.

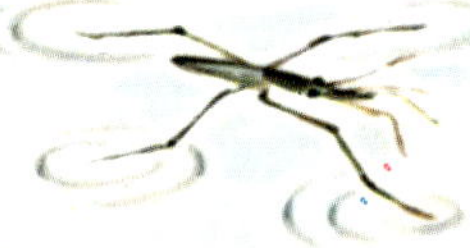

gerris
The skater or water-bug is funny to watch, darting every which way on the surface of the water.

anas platyrhynchos

The mallard duck with a blue-green head and his less colorful mate are migratory birds; in the Spring, they come to the northern pond to raise their ducklings, and in the Autumn they fly south to warmer weather.

equisetum

The horse tail is a plant that, millions of years ago, grew as high as a poplar tree. Now its rough and prickly stem does not grow more than a few feet tall.

This charming book also comes in a poster version, ready to brighten a child's wall. Your bookseller has it as well as others of the series.

illustration
Gerda Muller

text
Résie Pouyanne

adaptation
Suzy Patterson

design
Michel Cartacheff

Butterfly Books

TWO CONTINENTS PUBLISHING GROUP
30 East 42 Street, New York, New York 10017